The Kids' Invention Book

The Kids' Invention Book

by Arlene Erlbach

Lerner Publications Company
Minneapolis

To Martha, for making one invention into a venture

This book would not have been possible without
the generous help of the following people:
Ms. Ruth Ann Nybold, Ms. Ellen Cardwell, Mr. Nicholas Parnello,
Mr. Clayton E. Schulze, Dr. Edward Sobey, Dr. Leonard Molotsky,
Ms. Evie Andrews, Ms. Marion Canedo, Mr. Irv Siegelman.

The publisher would like to thank Dylan Crepps, Jade Crepps, Kim Rogness,
Jill Stenberg, and Alyssa Tuma, who were photographed for this book.

Series Editor: Martha Brennecke
Series Designer: Zachary Marell
Photographer: Nancy Smedstad
Electronic Prepress: Mike Kohn and Sean Todd

Copyright © 1997 by Arlene Erlbach

Library of Congress Cataloging-in-Publication Data

Erlbach, Arlene.
   The kids' invention book / by Arlene Erlbach.
     p.   cm.
   Includes index.
   Summary: Profiles eleven inventors between the ages of eight and fourteen,
describes the steps involved in inventing a new product, and discusses contests,
patents, lawyers, and clubs.
   ISBN 0-8225-2414-7 (alk. paper)
   1. Inventions—Juvenile literature. 2. Children as inventors—Juvenile
literature. [1. Inventions. 2. Children as inventors. 3. Inventors.] I. Title.
   T339.E75   1997
   608-dc20   96-27105

Manufactured in the United States of America
1 2 3 4 5 6 – JR – 02 01 00 99 98 97

1/99 Z006 18 12 |9. 2|

CONTENTS

Kids Are Inventors, Too

earmuffs

Do you know what's unusual about earmuffs? They were invented by a kid!

Chester Greenwood wanted to keep his ears warm, so he invented earmuffs. They solved a problem for him. That's what inventions are supposed to do. Chester's invention made life easier for millions of other people.

You may already be an inventor, too, without even knowing it. You're an inventor every time you

What is this thing? Is it a spring? It's a Slinky.®

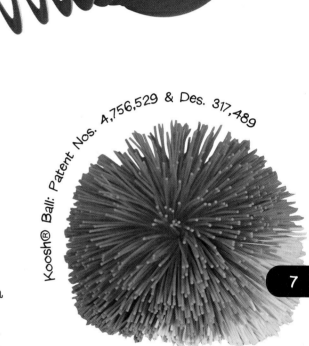

Koosh® Ball: Patent Nos. 4,756,529 & Des. 317,489

find a new way of doing something.

Have you ever made up new rules for a game? Or maybe you've wiped your mouth on your sleeve when you couldn't find a napkin. Your parents may not have been thrilled when they saw you do that, but you solved a problem for yourself.

Inventions are discoveries. An invention might be a new item, like the Koosh® Ball or Slinky® were when they first appeared in stores, years ago. Or an invention may improve something that already exists.

Think about your TV. You probably see color pictures on the screen. But the first TV sets showed only black-and-white pictures. The person who invented color television improved something that people were already using.

Chester Greenwood, as an adult, still wearing his "Champion Ear Protectors"

Let's go back to earmuffs. They were invented in 1873, when Chester Greenwood was only 15 years old.

Chester lived in Farmington, Maine, and he loved to ice skate. Anyone familiar with northeastern winters knows how hard they can be on your ears—even when you wear a hat. So Chester took a piece of wire and asked his grandmother to sew cloth pads on the ends.

At first Chester's friends thought his earmuffs looked weird, but they soon changed their minds. Chester could stay outside and skate longer than they did. His ears didn't get cold!

Soon Chester's friends wanted earmuffs, too. So he started making

Greenwood
Residents dress

By Donna Arsenault
FARMINGTON - Chester Greenwood Day originally welcomed winter on Dec. 21, the first day of the season.

Events for the day were rescheduled to the first Saturday in December because it was too cold when Dec. 21 rolled around.

But if you asked anyone attending this year's events on Saturday, they would have told you it felt like winter.

The clock at the corner of Main Street and Broadway read 19 degrees but the freezing wind made it feel much colder.

People were dressed appropriately, winter coats, scarves, mittens,

Fighting The Wind -

earmuffs and selling them. He also applied for a patent. A patent is a document issued by the U.S. government. It protects an inventor's idea so nobody else can make money from it. To learn more about patents, see Chapter 5.

Chester began manufacturing earmuffs and eventually became rich. He became famous, too. Farmington, Maine, celebrates Chester Greenwood Day each December.

Lots of kids—about 500,000 each year—invent things. Most kids don't sell their inventions or become rich. But they do have fun creating things and seeing them work.

Many of these children enter contests. Some of them win prizes. This book will tell you how you can enter these contests. You will learn how your ideas can become inventions that work.

Now meet the kids who have already done it.

Day parade welcomes winter
ppropriately and give a warm welcome

Chester Greenwood Day

de goers fought the wind during the Chester Greenwood Day Parade.

Parade-goers wear earmuffs in Chester Greenwood's honor—and to keep their ears warm—at the winter parade in Farmington, Maine.

Meet the Inventors

Inventor:
Suzanna Goodin
Hometown:
Hydro, Oklahoma

The Edible Pet-Food Spoon

Feeding a cat canned food is a messy job. First you dig the spoon into that smelly stuff. Then you shake the goop into a dish. The worst part is yet to come—washing off the spoon. Yuck!

Six-year-old Suzanna Goodin felt that way, too. She loved her cats, Ginger and Cinnamon, but she hated to feed them. Then Suzanna's teacher told her class about an invention contest they could enter. The teacher told the students that they should think about a problem to solve.

Suzanna thought about her problem with the cat food. She figured the best solution would be to design a special spoon—a spoon that the cats

Suzanna, at six, and her spoon

Yuck! Suzanna's inspiration

could eat would do the job. It could be dumped into the bowl with the food. That way, there would be no spoon left to clean up.

As simple as the idea seems, the spoon wasn't easy to make. The spoon needed to be strong enough and big enough to scoop the cat food from a can. It also had to be chewable.

Suzanna found a simple recipe for homemade dog biscuits, shaped the dough into spoons, and baked them in the oven. Then with the help of her grandmother, Suzanna tried various flavors. They thought a bit of added charcoal might help control "cat breath." One with brewer's yeast would offer extra vitamins. The final flavor decision was garlic, because the cats liked that taste and smell best.

Suzanna's cat food spoon won the contest prize. After she won the prize, many people thought Suzanna and her family might go into the edible pet-food spoon business. They didn't. An edible pet-food spoon takes lots of time to make. Each one must be shaped by hand. Making spoons to sell would have meant going into the baking business full-time.

Suzanna still wants to be an inventor when she grows up—but not an inventor of pet supplies.

"I want to be a fashion designer," she says.

A fashion designer is really an inventor—of clothes.

The Prosthetic Catch & Throw Device

Inventor:
Josh Parsons
Hometown:
Houston, Texas

JOSH

Josh Parsons wanted to help David Potter play baseball. Both of David's arms had been amputated below the elbows because of an accident he had had when he was two years old. Still, David wanted to be on a Little League team. Josh thought he could help David.

Josh's dad is the one who told Josh about David. Mr. Parsons is a Little League director. He judges kids' tryouts for teams. One evening, Mr. Parsons came home and told Josh about a kid without hands who had tried out for a baseball team.

Even without hands, David could catch and bat a ball! He caught the ball in a glove he wore at the end of his left arm. To bat, David held the bat between his left upper arm and chest. He used his right arm to push the bat. The only thing David couldn't do was throw a ball. Josh hoped he could change that.

First Josh thought about all the things David could already do. David was able to use a glove to catch. So maybe a special kind of glove could help him throw.

Josh decided to design a special glove that would replace David's lower right arm and hand. A device that replaces a missing body part is called a prosthesis (pross-THEE-sis).

Josh drew pictures of baseball gloves. Finally, he came up with a glove shaped like a scoop. Josh felt that this shape would allow David to both hold and then throw the ball.

Josh first made a model of the glove out of paper. Next, he sewed a glove from leather. The glove fit onto the end of David's right arm.

Josh hit a ball to David. David caught it in his left glove. Then he dumped the ball into the prosthetic glove and threw the ball into the air!

David started playing right field for the Spring Branch Mustangs. They won first place that season.

Josh's invention drew a lot of attention. He and David were interviewed on *Good Morning America* and the Cable News Network. Stories about the glove appeared in newspapers across the United States. Josh received an award from the Easter Seal Society, an organization that helps people with disabilities. He and David even threw out the first pitch at a Houston Astros game.

DAVID

Josh also received a prize from the Houston Inventors' Association— a 291-piece tool kit. He can make plenty of things with that. But, Josh says, "The most important part was that the glove helped David. That's why I invented it."

MS. ANGEL STELLO &
MS. KATHRYN MITCHELL
RR 1
HANAHAN, SC 29406

The Two-Door Mailbox

Inventors:
Angel Stello and
Kathryn Mitchell

Hometown:
Hanahan, South Carolina

In most cities and towns, mailboxes are attached to people's houses. But in some suburban and rural areas, people's houses are located far from main roads. People who live in these areas use rural route mailboxes.

Rural route mailboxes are mounted on stands near the street. These boxes make delivering mail faster and easier, because mail carriers can deliver mail from their trucks. But rural route boxes aren't always safe. With cars and trucks whizzing down roads, people can be injured when they pick up their mail.

Fifth graders Kathryn Mitchell and Angel Stello heard about a little kid who was hurt while taking mail out of a box. So Kathryn and Angel knew exactly what they wanted to invent for their school's invention contest—a mailbox with two doors. One door would be near the street, as usual, for the mail carrier to use. But the other door would open on the other side. With this kind of box, people wouldn't need to walk onto the road to get their mail.

Angel and Kathryn knew they'd need two mailboxes to make the two-door mailbox. They planned to cut the end off one box. They'd cut the door from the second mailbox. Then they'd screw the door from the second box onto the first box's open end.

Angel & Kathy, ready to get the mail

The process involved using a metal cutter and a drill. Kathryn and Angel's dads thought the girls were too young to use power tools. So Mr. Mitchell and Mr. Stello put the box together.

Once the second door was attached, Angel and Kathryn painted the mailbox with their names and address. On one side of the mailbox they painted "Angel–Kathy." On the other side they wrote "Kathy–Angel." This way, both girls got top billing.

The two-doored mailbox won an invention contest for their school. Next, it won a prize for the best kid's invention in South Carolina that year. The girls won a free trip to Washington, D.C., to visit an inventors' fair.

Angel and Kathryn thought of getting their two-door mailbox patented. Kathryn's father checked to see if a similar mailbox had been invented yet. He learned that thousands of patents for mailboxes had already been filed, and that some of the boxes were like Angel and Kathryn's.

Still, Kathryn and Angel received plenty of attention. They got a letter of congratulation from their state representative, and from the U.S. postmaster—the person in charge of mail for the entire United States. And the postmaster of South Carolina sent them each a T-shirt decorated with the state seal.

Drawing by Angel & Kathy

Drawing by Eric Bunnelle

Inventor:
Eric Bunnelle
Hometown:
Columbia, Missouri

Dial-a-Fish

"I wanted goldfish," says Eric Bunnelle. "My mom refused—unless I could find a way to feed them when we went on vacation."

Around the time Eric begged for fish, his teacher asked him to invent something. Eric decided to invent a remote-control fish feeder. This invention would take care of the problem with his mother and the school assignment, too.

Eric plugged an electrical massager into a telephone jack (the wall outlet for a phone). Then he clamped the massager to a stand that held a container of fish food. When Eric dialed his phone number—plus a special code—from outside the house, the massager would receive electrical current from the phone jack. The massager would shake the stand and shake food into a fish bowl.

"The first try was a dud," Eric says. "There wasn't enough power from the phone outlet, so the massager didn't shake."

Eric's mother took him to Radio Shack, an electronics store, to discuss the problem. The people at Radio Shack thought the fish feeder could work. Eric needed a "Fone Flasher," they said. That's a special telephone attachment for

people who are hearing-impaired. A Fone Flasher turns on a lamp when the phone rings. Eric could use a Fone Flasher to turn on the massager instead of a lamp.

Eric's mom bought the Fone Flasher. They plugged it into the phone jack at home. Then Eric plugged the Fone Flasher into the massager with the fish food container attached. When the phone rang, the massager worked!

But there was still a big problem. The massager didn't tilt the fish food container far enough to shake enough food into the fish bowl. Eric worked on this problem with an empty aquarium until he got the tilt just right. Getting it right took more than 20 tries.

Eric's remote-control fish feeder won a grand prize at a national contest for kids' inventions. Eric appeared on David Letterman's late-night talk show, too.

Eric even did a "market survey" to see if people would buy his invention. He spent an afternoon standing outside a pet store, asking fish owners if they would buy a remote-control fish feeder. He also asked how much they would pay for it. Most people said they'd pay up to $39.95.

Eric hasn't patented his fish feeder yet. It's expensive to do. But he has convinced his mother to let him have fish—and he's learned that persistence is important to success.

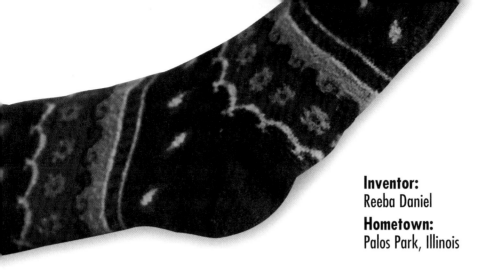

Inventor:
Reeba Daniel
Hometown:
Palos Park, Illinois

The All-in-One Washer/Dryer

"I wanted to design an automatic rabbit feeder for my school invention project," Reeba Daniel said. "But my teacher told me that automatic pet feeders had already been invented."

Then Reeba's mom gave her a suggestion. "Invent something everyone could use—something that saves time."

A few days later, Reeba was folding laundry. She thought about how doing laundry is a two-step job. First the clothes go into the washer. Then, when they're damp and heavy, somebody needs to lift them into the dryer. Reeba thought about inventing a machine that would wash and dry clothes in one step.

Reeba began drawing pictures. Her first idea involved placing the washer and dryer side by side. A conveyor belt would move the clothes from the washer to the dryer. The idea certainly seemed useful—but too complicated! It would also be very expensive to manufacture.

Reeba thought of a simpler way to make her idea work. The washer could be on top of the dryer. Her washer would have a trapdoor that would open following the

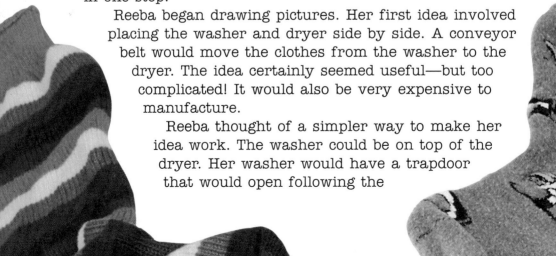

drain cycle. The clothes would drop into the dryer, making it start. A computerized device could time each of the cycles.

Reeba didn't make a working model of her invention. It would have cost thousands of dollars to build. Instead, she did what many inventors do: Reeba drew a diagram of her invention. Then she made a model of it, from cardboard. From her diagram and model, people could see how her invention would look.

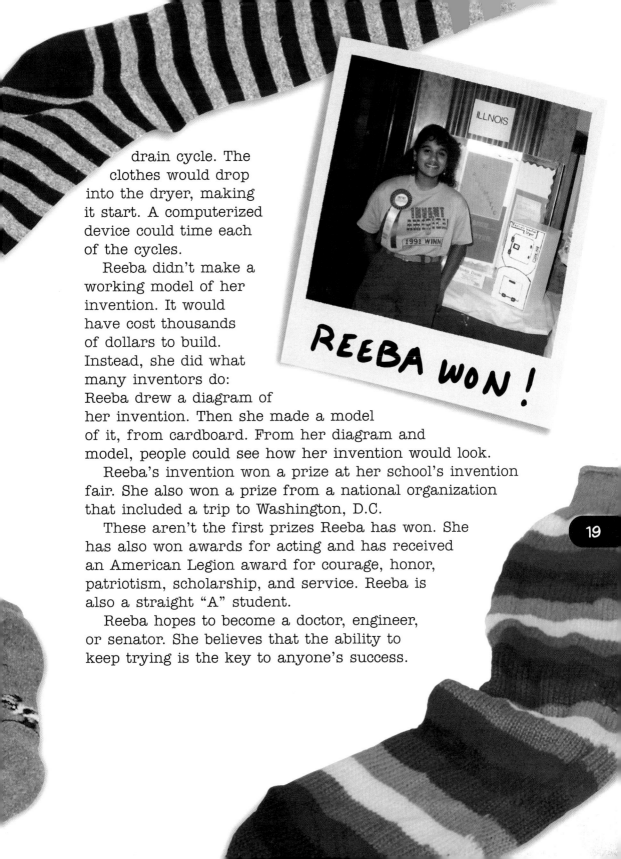

REEBA WON!

Reeba's invention won a prize at her school's invention fair. She also won a prize from a national organization that included a trip to Washington, D.C.

These aren't the first prizes Reeba has won. She has also won awards for acting and has received an American Legion award for courage, honor, patriotism, scholarship, and service. Reeba is also a straight "A" student.

Reeba hopes to become a doctor, engineer, or senator. She believes that the ability to keep trying is the key to anyone's success.

The Adjustable
Jump-Rope Belt

Big and Small, Short and Tall,
One or More, It Fits All!

That's the poem enclosed in Jessica Peach's adjustable jump-rope package. She has sold hundreds of jump ropes—and business keeps improving.

Jessica first thought about a new kind of jump rope during gym class. Her gym teacher, Ms. Hansen, loves to teach jump rope. She teaches about a hundred different games.

Different games need different lengths of rope. So every time Jessica and her friends wanted to change games, they'd have to switch ropes. Jessica wanted to make changing ropes simpler. She thought it would be easier to use one jump rope that could be made long or short.

It's stylish, too.

Jessica decided to design a jump rope made of two seven-foot pieces of rope connected by loose knots. Kids could pull one piece through the knots' holes to lengthen the rope.

Jessica thought of another use for her jump rope. When kids finished playing, they could wrap it around their waists and braid it into a belt. Jessica thought the rope could come in different colors, to match clothes.

First Jessica used plastic clothesline to make the jump rope. That didn't work. The plastic was flimsy and didn't absorb the dye she used to try to color it. Next she tried cotton clothesline. She made a small sample, first for a Barbie doll. The tiny jump rope looked good. Then Jessica made an adjustable jump rope to fit herself.

Jessica's in business.

Jessica had one problem with her adjustable jump rope—the ends frayed. If the ends kept fraying, the adjustable jump rope wouldn't last very long.

Jessica needed something to hold the jump rope's ends together. First she tried metal end sleeves, tubes that plumbers use to seal pipes. That worked, but the sleeves were hard to put on. They were also expensive.

Jessica experimented next with dipping the rope ends into hot glue. The glue burned the ends and held them together. Then she went to a craft store and bought decorative metal caps called bolo caps. She put the bolo caps over the glued ends of the rope.

The adjustable jump rope was a hit. It won a national invention contest and toy stores bought it. Jessica might sell her adjustable-jump-rope idea to a toy company. She has applied for a patent, too.

Jessica has other inventions as well. She has invented animal-shaped teapots with two spouts. And she has invented a privacy shield, a sheet of heavy plastic that keeps kids from snooping in other kids' desks at school!

21

Bolo cap

Inventor:
Kevin Germino
Hometown:
Palatine, Illinois

Mr. Fishy's Neighborhood

Kevin Germino loves to fish. When he goes fishing with his grandfather, they see lures floating on the water. Lures fall off people's lines, or escaping fish pull the lures off. Sometimes people carelessly throw them away. The metal and plastic pollute the water.

Looking at the lures on a lake one day, Kevin got an idea. Why not invent a biodegradable fishing lure? Biodegradable items break down into harmless products. If a biodegradable lure were lost or tossed away, the lure would dissolve in water.

Kevin knew exactly how he wanted his lure to look—like a candy gummy worm. But this gummy worm would be for fish, not kids. The lure had to be stronger than a candy gummy worm. It needed to last for a while in the water, at least long enough to catch some fish.

Kevin's grandfather is a chemist. His job involves showing companies how to design food. Kevin's grandfather gave him advice about ingredients. He told Kevin to use xanthan gum, algin, and carageenan gum.

These three ingredients are used in many foods we eat. When you eat candies such as gummy worms or gummy bears, they often have xanthan gum in them. That's what makes them jellylike. Carageenan gum gives the ingredients shape. Algin makes all the ingredients stick together.

Kevin's lure would need two

Gummys are yummy

Kevin catches on.

more ingredients: a color and a flavor to attract fish. Kevin already knew from experience that fish like bright colors and that they like the flavor of malt. Kevin decided to add orange food coloring and malt to his recipe.

Kevin's first step was to prepare a mold. He poured plaster of paris into a glass, then dropped in a worm-shaped plastic fishing lure. He removed the lure, which left an impression in the plaster of paris. When Kevin poured his mixed ingredients into this mold, they would form in the shape of the lure.

Getting the right mix of ingredients was the hard part. Kevin tried 14 combinations before he got the mixture to harden the way he wanted it to. Sometimes the lures cracked after they came out of the mold. Sometimes the texture was wrong. Finally, Kevin added a little more xanthan gum and water. It worked!

Kevin just needed a name for his invention. One kid in Kevin's class joked that he should name it "Mr. Fishy's Neighborhood." The name sounded silly, but it also sounded right.

Mr. Fishy's Neighborhood won a school invention contest. Kevin also entered his invention in another contest, but it didn't win that time. A girl who invented a talking measuring cup won.

Whether Kevin wins any more prizes or not, he's still glad he invented Mr. Fishy. He learned a lot.

Inventor:
Larry Villella
Hometown:
Fargo, North Dakota

The Conserve Sprinkler

One of Larry Villella's chores was watering the lawn, which included watering eight trees and eight shrubs.

He had to hose each tree and shrub separately or keep moving the sprinkler around.

Larry thought he was wasting a lot of water every time he would change the sprinkler or move the hose. He thought a sprinkler that actually fit around a tree or shrub would save water—and time. And the plant would get more water if the sprinkler had holes on the top *and* bottom.

Larry believed a circular sprinkler could do the trick. He'd just need to cut an opening in the sprinkler so it would fit

Larry's sprinkler in action

Larry's a
businessman, too.

THE CONSERVE
SPRINKLER
1-800-EARTH 37

around a tree or shrub. Then he'd need to seal the ends.

Larry and his dad cut a section from a sprinkler with a power saw. They sealed the ends by gluing on pieces of thin plastic. Then they drilled holes in the bottom of the sprinkler that were wider than the tiny holes on top. The bigger holes would allow water to seep into the ground and soak the plant's roots.

Larry's sprinkler won his school's invention contest. Then he and his dad showed it to Dr. Ron Smith, a professor of agriculture at North Dakota State University. Dr. Smith suggested a change. He thought the holes on the bottom should be even bigger, so more water would go into the ground and aerate (supply air to) the soil.

25

Larry began making Conserve Sprinklers by hand and selling them. They sold so well that Larry didn't have time to make them all. At first, he turned the manufacturing over to a training center for people who are handicapped. But sales grew even more, and Larry needed a place that could mass produce the sprinklers. A company called Terhorst in Minot, North Dakota, began manufacturing them, and thousands of people have bought Larry's sprinklers.

Inventor:
Alison DeSmyter
Hometown:
Houston, Texas

The Rampanion

Alison DeSmyter knows about the problems people have in wheelchairs. Alison was born with cerebral palsy, a condition that makes it difficult to control muscles. So Alison has used a wheelchair most of her life.

One common problem for wheelchair users is crossing streets with curbs. To get her chair over a curb, Alison needed somebody to push or lift her chair. She wanted more independence. So Alison invented the Rampanion—a portable ramp that allows a wheelchair to move easily over a curb.

Alison first thought of the Rampanion when she was asked to do an invention project for school. She had just two weeks. That wasn't much time to design something as complicated as the Rampanion. But Alison did it! First Alison thought about making a rubber ramp, but she decided it would be too bulky to carry around. Next she considered an inflatable ramp. That wouldn't do, either—it would always need to be blown up. Finally Alison decided to make a ramp out of lightweight metal. This type of ramp could easily be folded and carried.

Alison began by building a small model of her ramp from Popsicle sticks. Once she had built the model, she

Alison did it!

26

First Alison got down to nuts and bolts.

thought about the type of metal she'd use for the real thing. The Rampanion needed to be light yet strong, so Alison decided on aluminum. Her father found some aluminum where he works, and he helped Alison put the ramp together. To build the ramp, they needed a lot of exact measurements, which Alison took herself.

As Alison and her father built the Rampanion, they thought of improvements they could make to its design. They added an edge to the Rampanion's sides, to keep a chair's wheels on track. They put sticky tape on the bottom, to help secure the Rampanion to any surface—even in the rain.

The completed Rampanion weighs only four pounds. When it's folded, it can be carried in its own cloth bag. The bag can be attached to a wheelchair.

Alison's Rampanion won the fifth grade grand prize for the third annual Houston Inventors' Showcase Exposition. Her prize was a trip to Florida. The trip included visits to Disneyworld, the Kennedy Space Center, and Thomas Edison's estate. Thomas Edison was a great inventor who created many electrical devices, such as the light bulb and the phonograph.

Alison hasn't stopped inventing things for wheelchair users. She's working on a Handy Helper, which is a tray that attaches to a wheelchair. The Handy Helper allows people in wheelchairs to be served more easily in cafeterias and fast-food restaurants.

Inventor:
Robbie Marcucci
Hometown:
Tualatin, Oregon

The Crayon Saver

Drawing by Robbie Marcucci

Like most kids, Robbie Marcucci loves to color. And, of course, his crayons always break or wear down. Then they are too short to use because they can't be held easily. Robbie calls these short crayons "nubbies." Between Robbie and his sister, they had a whole can of nubbies. Nobody ever used them.

Robbie wanted to figure out a way to use the nubbies. They were perfectly good. They just needed some sort of holder that would make them longer. Then they wouldn't be wasted.

Robbie thought about a holder that would work like a push-up pop does. He could put the nubbie inside a thin paper tube, cut to the length of a crayon, and something would push it up. A paper drinking straw is about the width of a crayon, so Robbie thought that it would make a perfect holder. A short screw pushed inside the straw could move the crayon up.

Crayon saver
Robbie M.

The paper straw didn't work as well as Robbie had expected. The crayon got stuck, or the straw ripped. Finally, Robbie made a discovery. The straw from a sports bottle is a little wider than a paper straw. Since it's made from plastic, it's stronger, too. A plastic crayon holder would last a long time.

Robbie's teacher, Mrs. Andrews, thought Robbie's Crayon Saver was a hit. Not only had he found a way to keep from wasting crayons, he'd designed something that a lot of kids would like to use. Robbie's Crayon Saver won a blue ribbon at his school invention fair.

As part of his school's invention program, Robbie and his class learned about patents. Mrs. Andrews gave Robbie a mock patent for the Crayon Saver.

Robbie never really considered patenting the Crayon Saver or trying to sell it. But somebody else did! About a year after he invented his Crayon Saver, Robbie and his family saw an article in their local paper about an almost identical product. Robbie was shocked and disappointed. He wonders if the manufacturer copied his invention.

Robbie is not inventing anymore. He's a state champion gymnast, so he's putting his energy into other activities.

Inventor:
Matthew Erlbach
Hometown:
Morton Grove, Illinois

The Nappy Shirt

Matthew Erlbach loved to wipe his face on his shirtsleeve at restaurants. Napkins in restaurants are often flimsy and thin. A shirt sleeve is much thicker and stronger. It did a better job.

Matt's parents always told him that wiping his mouth on his sleeve was disgusting. It also made spots on his shirt. Still, Matt didn't think there was a better alternative.

"NEED A NAPKIN, MATT?"

This problem gave Matt an idea. He could invent a shirt with a napkin attached to it. If he could take the napkin off, he could throw it in the laundry later or throw the napkin away. All he needed was a way to attach the napkin to the shirt. He also had to decide what type of napkin would work best—cloth or heavy paper.

First, Matt attached Velcro tabs to a long-sleeved T-shirt. He also sewed Velcro tabs to a cloth napkin. The napkin held on to the shirt. This wasn't a very good solution, though. It worked when he wiped his mouth, but it was annoying to try to replace. Once Matt left the napkin at the restaurant and had to go back for it. The next time he wanted to use the napkin, it was in the wash.

Matt wondered if a heavy paper napkin might work better. He could throw the napkin away when he was done using it. But the paper napkin created another problem. The napkin tore when Matt sewed on the Velcro.

Finally, Matt developed a different way to hold the napkin to his shirt. He sewed bands of elastic to the shirt's sleeve. He sewed them tight enough to hold the napkin in place. Now he has a shirt that holds a napkin that can be thrown out.

Matt is still thinking of other things to invent. He hasn't gotten around to inventing them yet. He'd like to design an antipollution machine and bubble gum that never loses its flavor.

Or maybe, he says, "I'd like to be a comedian. I'd be inventing ways to make people laugh."

"NOPE."

Inventor:
Jeanie Low
Hometown:
Houston, Texas

The Kiddie Stool

Patent number 5,094,515 is an unusual one. It belongs to Jeanie Low. At age 10, Jeanie was the youngest American female to receive a patent. She received it for her foldaway Kiddie Stool.

Jeanie invented the Kiddie Stool when she was only five. Like many little kids, Jeanie used a stool to help her reach the bathroom sink. Jeanie lived in a house with a small bathroom, so her stool often got in the way. Family members accidentally kicked it around. Finally, the stool broke.

Jeanie needed a stool that would always be there but could be kept out of the way. She decided to invent one. She thought about a stool that would attach to the cabinet door under the bathroom sink.

Jeanie

Next, Jeanie thought about exactly how the stool would work. The stool could be made from two pieces of wood connected by metal hinges. The hinges would make the stool fold. She'd attach magnets to the bathroom cabinet door. When the stool folded up, the metal hinges would hit the magnets. The stool would stick to the cabinet door.

Jeanie drew a diagram of her stool. Then, she and her dad took the drawing to a hardware store to buy the materials she needed. The people at the store said it wouldn't work. They didn't think the magnets could hold a folded stool to the cabinet door.

Other people's opinions didn't stop Jeanie or her dad. Jeanie put the stool together with her dad's help. It worked fine. Jeanie called her invention the Kiddie Stool, and she entered it in her school's invention fair and contest. The Kiddie Stool won an honorable mention.

One of Jeanie's father's friends thought Jeanie had a great idea—one that would sell. So Jeanie got a patent.

Now people can buy the stool ready-made or in a kit to put together themselves. Jeanie's parents are trying to sell the Kiddie Stool to builders to install in new homes.

Jeanie also has invented a bathtub alarm that goes off when the water in the tub is going to overflow. She's designed a circular doormat, too. The mat attaches to the bottom of the door. It rotates in place as you rub mud off your shoes. Jeanie is trying to get patents on these inventions, too.

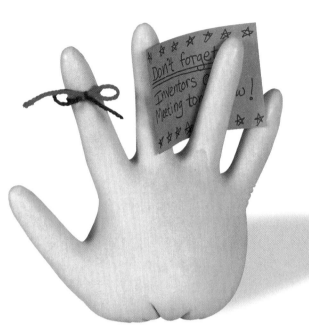

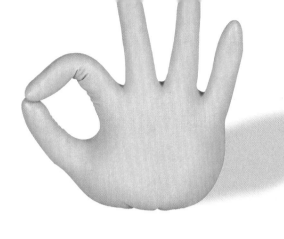

Inventor:
Elizabeth Low
Hometown:
Houston, Texas

The Happy Hand

When Elizabeth Low was little, she loved to play at her dad's office. He's a doctor, and he has all kinds of interesting things lying around.

Give Elizabeth a hand for her invention!

One day at the office, Elizabeth noticed a surgical glove. She took it home and filled it with sand. It became a hand-shaped beanbag with fingers she moved around and played with. She called it the Happy Hand.

Elizabeth found other uses for her Happy Hand. It can be used as a paperweight. The fingers can be moved to hold business cards and reminders.

Elizabeth entered the Happy Hand in a school invention show. It won!

Then Elizabeth took the Happy Hand to a Houston inventors' fair. Lots of people were fascinated by it, especially adults. They enjoyed molding the hand into different poses. They thought the Happy Hand was useful and fun.

At age nine, Elizabeth Low received a patent for her invention. She took the place of her sister Jeanie as the youngest American female to receive a patent.

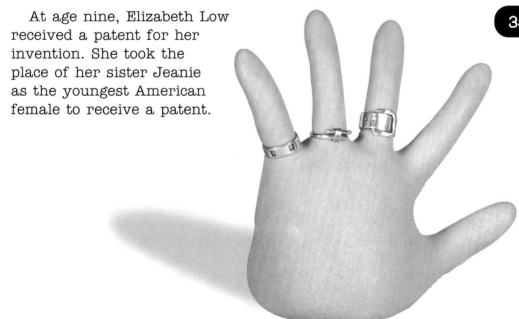

You Can Do It

When you invent, you think up ideas.
Then you make them work, step by step.

Steps to Creating an Invention

1 Think of ways to make life easier or better for you or people you know. Think of problems that need to be solved. Think about what goes on in your home or at school. Observe your friends, families, and pets. They may have problems you've never thought about before.

2 Make a list of these problems in a notebook.

All inventions start here.

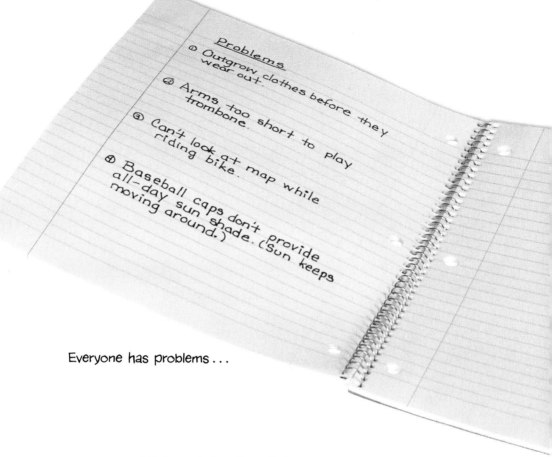

Problems

① Outgrow clothes before they wear out.

② Arms too short to play trombone.

③ Can't look at map while riding bike.

④ Baseball caps don't provide all-day sun shade. (Sun keeps moving around.)

Everyone has problems . . .

This notebook will be your invention journal. Whenever you think of another problem that needs solving, write about it in your journal. Some inventors take their journals with them wherever they go.

❸ From your list of problems, choose one that you think you can solve. Make sure it's one you find important and interesting enough to keep working on.

❹ Think about how to solve the problem. Lie down on your bed or sit in a comfortable chair. Think of lots of solutions to the problem. Some of them won't make any sense. Some will sound good. Some will seem absolutely terrific. This

process is called *brainstorming*. It allows you to come up
with many ideas, answers, and plans.

⑤ List the best solutions in your journal. Next, describe how
the solutions might look if you turned them into something
tangible—something you can see and touch.

⑥ Look over your solutions. Which one can you actually
make yourself—or with some adult help?

... and every problem has a
solution. Some are better than
others, of course.

38

...clothes before they

...s too short to play
...mbone.

...'t look at map while
...ding bike.

3aseball caps don't provide
...ll-day sun shade. (Sun keeps
moving around.)

Solutions

① a) Expandable clothes made from super-stretchy fabric.
   b) Sectional clothes— attach additional pieces as you grow.

② a) Hand-held slide mover extends arm length.
   b)

③ a) Scrolling map attaches to handlebars.
   b) Transparent map stickers to stick on back of sunglasses.

④ a) Sunhat based on baseball cap design with multiple, movable brims.

7 Once you've decided which solution you'll use, ask yourself these questions:

> *Is my invention really a new idea?*
> *Is it useful?*
> *Can it be made easily?*
> *Does it use materials that are easily available?*
> *Will it hold up after lots of use?*
> *And, will people really use it?*

If any of the answers to your questions are "no," think of how you might modify, or change, your idea. Inventors change ideas all the time.

8 Once all the answers to your questions are "yes," draw pictures of how your invention should look. You don't need to be a great artist to do this. Simple line drawings will do. Your first drawing is a rough draft. It shows the basic idea of what the invention will look like. A rough draft is meant to be changed.

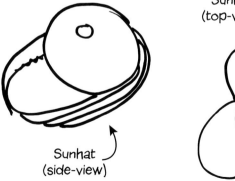

Sunhat
(side-view)

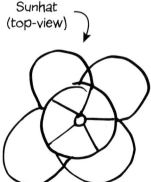

Sunhat
(top-view)

Your detailed drawings should show exactly how your invention works.

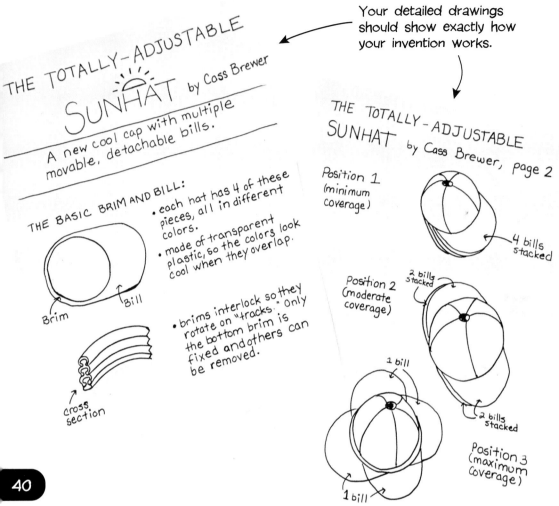

THE TOTALLY-ADJUSTABLE SUNHAT by Cass Brewer

A new cool cap with multiple movable, detachable bills.

THE BASIC BRIM AND BILL:

• each hat has 4 of these pieces, all in different colors.
• made of transparent plastic, so the colors look cool when they overlap.

Brim

Bill

cross section

• brims interlock so they rotate on "tracks." Only the bottom brim is fixed and others can be removed.

THE TOTALLY-ADJUSTABLE SUNHAT by Cass Brewer, page 2

Position 1 (minimum coverage)

4 bills stacked

Position 2 (moderate coverage)

2 bills stacked

2 bills stacked

1 bill

1 bill

Position 3 (maximum coverage)

9 Next, you need to refine the drawing of your invention. This means redrawing until it looks exactly right. Sometimes this process takes lots of tries. On your final drawing, label all the parts. On the back of your paper, list the materials you'll need to make your invention.

10 Now comes a very important step—building the model. You might need an adult to help you. That's okay. Lots of adult inventors pay people to make models for them. You may need to build your model more than once. Sometimes inventions don't work as you had hoped.

11 Once your model is exactly the way you want it, have some of your friends and relatives use it. Use it a few times yourself. Does it hold up and work? Congratulations! You've just created a new invention!

Invention Contests

Kids are offered many opportunities to enter invention contests. Some of the best-known groups that sponsor contests are Silver Burdett & Ginn, and The Network for Inventive Thinkers. Each contest has different rules and prizes.

Cognetics National Talent Network

This organization offers certificates to groups seeking solutions to problems.

Cognetics National Talent Network
700 Holly Dell Court
Sewell, NJ 08080
(609) 582-7000

The Great Idea Contest

The Great Idea Contest is held each year for students of all ages.

Inventors Workshop
International Education Foundation (IWIEF)
3201 Corte Malpaso, #304-A
Camarillo, CA 93010
(818) 998-7404 or (805) 484-9786

Network for Inventive Thinkers

This organization offers conferences, conventions, and contests for creative kids.

Network for Inventive Thinkers
Commissioner of Patents and Trademarks
Public Affairs
Washington, DC 20231
(703) 305-8341

43

Odyssey of the Mind

This association organizes competitions for groups of five to seven kids who solve problems using teamwork. It awards trophies, plaques, certificates, medals, and scholarships. To enter a competition, you must attend a school or belong to a community organization that is an OM member.

Odyssey of the Mind
P.O. Box 27
Glassboro, NJ 08028
(609) 881-1603

Winning Tips

Everyone wants his or her invention to be a winner. Here are tips to help you receive top ratings from teachers and judges.

1. Make sure all your paperwork is neat, including the application and all diagrams. If you have poor handwriting, type your forms or have someone type them for you, if the rules allow.

2. Follow all contest rules and directions exactly.

3. Keep your design simple. Complicated items with lots of parts don't usually win. The extra parts detract from the invention's purpose.

4. Make sure your invention is something people would really use.

5. Slightly humorous inventions appeal to judges. Remember the Edible Pet-Food Spoon and Mr. Fishy's Neighborhood? These things are useful, yet they bring a smile to people.

6. Judges tend to like inventions for pets.

7. Inventions designed for handicapped people appeal to judges and teachers, too. This shows that you used your problem-solving skills to help people who have special needs.

8. Judges also like inventions that are good for or protect the environment. What's good for the environment is good for everyone.

Silver Burdett & Ginn Invention Contest

To enter this contest, your school must use the Silver Burdett & Ginn Contest science program. Many schools do. Each school must conduct a local invention contest. The winners of school contests become eligible for the Silver Burdett & Ginn International Invention Convention. Students in grades 1 through 9 may participate.

200 ft.

150 ft.

Patents

Once you've created an invention, you might be afraid that somebody will steal your idea.

You can protect your idea with something called a *patent*. A patent is a document issued by the United States government. It gives the person who has it, and that person only, the right to make that item and sell it. But a patent is very expensive and you may not really need one. Applying for a patent is something to think over carefully.

There are three kinds of patents—utility patents, design patents, and plant patents.

Utility Patents. Utility patents apply to all mechanical and electrical devices. Most things you invent will probably fall into this category. The government grants more utility patents than any other kind.

100 ft.

Can you patent a kite? You can if your kite is different from any other.

Design Patents. These patents apply to original designs for already existing products. Let's say you invented a sneaker-shaped pen. Somebody already invented pens, but your pen design would be new. The patent for your sneaker-shaped pen would fall into the design patent category.

Plant Patents. These patents apply to unique breeds of plants. If you developed a way to grow a 200-foot sunflower, you'd be eligible to apply for a plant patent.

To receive a patent, your invention must be useful and new. Most inventions pass easily on usefulness.

But the patent office is strict about the item being new. For your invention to be new, you must be the absolute first person to invent that item. You must be the first person to show the invention to anybody or show a description of it to anyone. For example, let's pretend somebody designed a glow-in-the-dark kite in China 500 years ago, and you invented one, too. If that original inventor showed the kite to other people—or even wrote a description of it—your kite can't be patented. It doesn't matter if the item was ever manufactured or used.

Once you display or have stories written about your invention, you have a year to apply for a patent. After that, your invention is no longer patentable. Anyone can read the article about your invention and manufacture it.

Applying for a Patent

People usually see a lawyer or a patent agent when they think about applying for a patent. Lawyers and patent agents often give free first appointments. At the appointment, they will give you an idea of what the patent process will cost. Sometimes they may even tell you prices over the phone.

Both lawyers and patent agents charge a lot for their services. They can charge from $500 to many thousands of dollars. These fees are in addition to filing, issue, and maintenance fees charged by the government.

The first step in filing a patent is to complete a patent search. You will need to look through patents in your category to see if an item like yours exists. This step can be done at a large library. If your local library doesn't keep patent records, a librarian there will know of one that does.

Once you find out your idea is original, you can fill out a patent application. You'll need a lawyer or patent agent for this process. When you meet with the lawyer or agent, you must bring all your diagrams and notes.

After the paperwork is complete, you sign it and it is mailed to the U.S. patent office in Washington, D.C. Experts at the patent office do another patent search, which can take from one to three years. You sometimes see products with the words *patent pending* on them. "Patent pending," or "pat pending," means that the inventor has not received the patent yet—the patent office is still doing a search. But

Patent
paperwork
piles up: So
be patient.

because the inventor has applied for
a patent, nobody can copy the invention.

If your application checks out, you'll be notified by mail.
Then you pay the fees, and you'll receive your patent on a
fancy gold-stamped sheet of paper. Your patent is assigned a
number. You must put this patent number on your invention.

Once you receive the patent, it's yours. Only you can
manufacture the item. You can sell your patent, lend it, or
rent it to anyone. A patent is good for 17 years. After that,

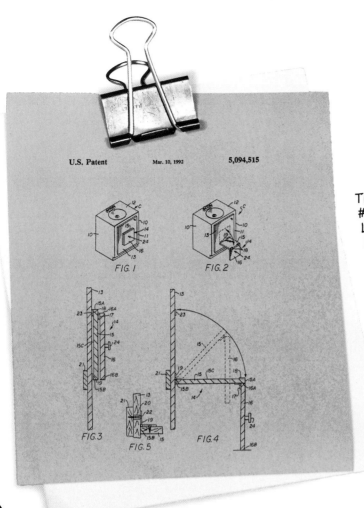

U.S. Patent — Mar. 10, 1992 — 5,094,515

FIG. 1 FIG. 2 FIG.3 FIG. 5 FIG. 4

This is U.S. Patent #5,094,515: Jeanie Low's patent for her Kiddie Stool.

anyone can manufacture your invention. During the time that your patent is valid, it's your job to make sure nobody steals your idea.

If you and your parents decide to patent or sell your invention, check with a lawyer or agent first. You may decide you don't want to patent your invention because of the high costs. Even if you don't have a patent, you can still make your item and sell it—if nobody else has a patent on an invention like yours.

Basic Patent Fees*

Filing Fee	**$365.00**
Patent Issue Fee	
(Paid only if patent is granted)	**$605.00**
Maintenance Fee	
(Paid 3½ years after original patent)	**$480.00**
Maintenance Fee	
(Paid 7½ years after original patent)	**$965.00**
Maintenance Fee	
(Paid 11½ years after original patent)	**$1450.00**

If you or your parents would like to know more about the patent process, contact:

> **Public Service Center**
> Patent and Trademark Office
> Washington, DC 20231
> (703) 305-8341

*1996 fees. Call the Patent and Trademark Office for the latest patent fees.

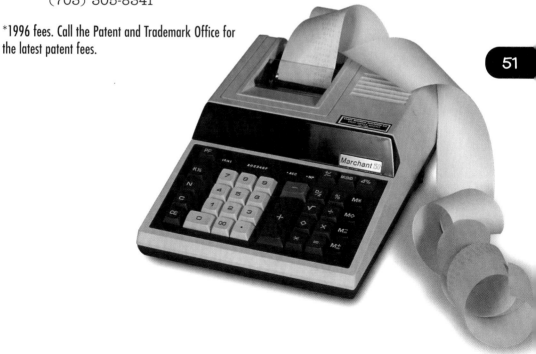

Start an Inventors' Club

An inventors' club is a great place to meet other kids interested in inventing. You can share ideas and invent things together.

The best place to start an inventors' club is at school. Discuss the idea with your classroom teacher or science teacher. Decide on a good time and place for your club to meet. Put up posters and design flyers to pass around. Announce the meeting of your inventors' club over the school loudspeaker.

Start an inventors' club at the beginning of the school year or about six weeks before your school's science or invention fair. Members can work on fair entries together and give each other tips for improvement.

Invite speakers to your meetings by contacting other local inventors' clubs. Sometimes speakers will appear free of charge or for a small fee. Some local inventors may be willing to help organize and judge contests.

If you don't want to start your own club, you may find an existing club you can join. Some inventors' clubs offer memberships to kids, for a small fee. On the next page is a list of associations you can contact. You don't need to live in a certain town to join any of them.

Inventors' Clubs

American Inventors' Council
Box 4304
Rockford, IL 61110

Houston Inventors' Association
2916 West T.C. Jester
Houston, TX 77018
(713) 686-7676

Inventors Clubs of America
P.O. Box 450261
Atlanta, GA 31145-0261
1-800-336-0169

The Inventors' Network
1445 Summit Street
Columbus, OH 43201
(614) 291-7900

**Inventors' Workshop
International**
3201 Corte Malpaso, #304-A
Camarillo, CA 93010

**The Pennsylvania
Inventors' Association**
8282 McKee Road
Albion, PA 16401
(814) 922-3000

An Invention Camp

Camp Invention offers a weeklong camp in many cities.
Programs are offered over the summer. Scholarships are
available to children whose families are unable to pay.

Camp Invention
National Invention Center
80 W. Bowery, Suite 201
Akron, OH 44308

More Information

For More Reading

Aaseng, Nathan. *The Inventors: Nobel Prizes in Chemistry, Physics, and Medicine.* Minneapolis: Lerner, 1988. (Grades 4 & up)

Bundles, A'Lella Perry. *Madam C. J. Walker.* New York: Chelsea House, 1991. (Grades 4 & up)

Dommermuth-Costa, Carol. *Nikola Tesla: A Spark of Genius.* Minneapolis: Lerner, 1994. (Grades 5 & up)

James, Portia P. *The Real McCoy: African-American Invention and Innovation, 1619–1930.* Washington, DC: Smithsonian Institution, 1989. (Grades 5 & up)

Macaulay, David. *The Way Things Work.* Boston: Houghton Mifflin, 1988. (Grades 4 & up)

Macdonald, Anne L. *Feminine Ingenuity: Women and Invention in America.* New York: Ballantine, 1992. (Grades 5 & up)

Mitchell, Barbara. *A Pocketful of Goobers: A Story about George Washington Carver.* Carolrhoda, 1986. (Grades 3–6)

Mitchell, Barbara. *The Wizard of Sound: A Story about Thomas Edison.* Minneapolis: Carolrhoda, 1991. (Grades 3–6)

Richardson, Robert O. *The Weird & Wondrous World of Patents.* New York: Sterling, 1990. (Grades 3 & up)

Stanley, Autumn. *Mothers and Daughters of Invention: Notes for a Revised History of Technology.* Metuchen, NJ: Scarecrow Press, 1993. (Grades 5 & up)

Swanson, Gloria M. and Margaret V. Ott. *I've Got an Idea! The Story of Frederick McKinley Jones.* Minneapolis: Runestone Press, Lerner Publishing Group, 1993. (Grades 3–6)

Other Resources

American Society of Inventors, Inc. (ASI)
P.O. Box 58426
Philadelphia, PA 19102-8426
(215) 546-6601

A nonprofit organization that works with government and industry to encourage invention and innovation. Sponsors educational programs.

American Society of Mechanical Engineers
22 Law Drive, Box 2900
Fairfield, NJ 07007-2900
1-800-843-2763

Sells a video called "The Mothers of Invention," which highlights the significant achievements of a dozen female and minority inventors. The video package includes a teacher's guide and poster.

Innovation Institute
901 South National Avenue, Box 88
Springfield, MO 65804-0089
(417) 836-5072

Evaluates inventions, assessing the market potential of new products, with the objective of creating new job opportunities in the United States.

Intellectual Property Owners (IPO)
1255 Twenty-third Street N.W., Suite 850
Washington, DC 20037
(202) 466-2396
Fax: (202) 466-2893

A nonprofit organization that represents people who own intellectual property (patents, copyrights, trademarks, and trade secrets). An annual fee entitles members to publications as well as invitations to meetings and conferences.

Inventure Place
The National Inventors Hall of Fame
221 South Broadway Street
Akron, OH 44308-1505
General information: 1-800-968-IDEA
Information about educational programs: (216) 762-6565
World Wide Web Site: http://www.invent.org./

Offers teacher training workshops, Saturday-morning kids'
workshops, and overnight camps for kids ages 6 & up and their
parents at the Akron location. Camp Invention, for grades 2-6, and
Camp Ingenuity, for grades 7-9, are day camps held in several cities
each year across the United States. Inventure Place houses
interactive exhibits. The National Inventors Hall of Fame pays
tribute to a diverse group of more than 100 inventors.

National Congress of Inventors Organizations (NCIO)
Los Angeles Office
(213) 878-6952

Coordinates information relating to inventor education and programs and keeps database of credible organizations who offer development and marketing assistance. Also offers children's services and educational programs.

National Inventive Thinking Association (NITA)
Living Resource Center
Houston Independent School District
11833 Chimney Rock
Houston, TX 77035

A nonprofit organization that collects and distributes instructional materials for creative thinking. Hosts an annual conference on developing critical thinking and problem-solving skills in children.

The National Women's History Project
7738 Bell Road, Dept. P
Windsor, CA 95492
(707) 838-6000

Offers a series of 12 colorful posters, geared toward fifth and sixth graders, on women inventors and their inventions. The series highlights inventions in numerous industries, including technology, medicine, business, domestic science, and agriculture.

U. S. Department of Commerce
Office of Patents and Trademarks
Washington, DC 20231
(703) 308-HELP

Evaluates patent applications and grants U.S. patents. The agency also provides information on obtaining patents and names of credible patent attorneys.

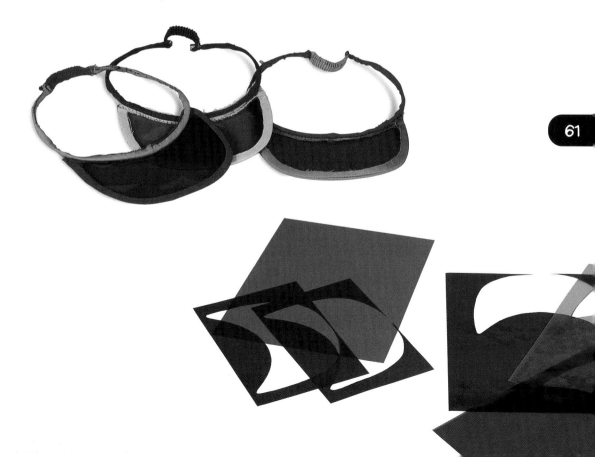

Glossary

brainstorming: a type of problem solving, in which ideas are shared freely and not immediately judged

market survey: a survey designed to determine if customers would buy a certain product

patent: a document that gives an inventor the right to make or sell an invention. A patent also prevents anyone except the inventor from making or selling the product.

patent pending: words printed on an object when a patent for the product has been applied for but not yet granted. Sometimes written as *pat pending.*

persistence: the ability to stick to an activity or idea, even though problems arise, without getting discouraged

rough draft: a version of sketch, drawing, or piece of writing that is in its first form. A rough draft is meant to be changed later.

tangible: real; capable of being touched

valid: in effect. A contract or patent that is valid is protected by law.

Index

63

About the Author

Arlene Erlbach has written more than 30 books of fiction and nonfiction for young people. Her book *Video Games* was a 1996 selection for the ALA's list of Quick Picks for Young Adults, a list of books recommended for reluctant young readers.

In addition to being an author, Ms. Erlbach is an elementary school teacher. She loves to encourage children to read and write, and she is in charge of her school's Young Authors' program. Ms. Erlbach lives in Morton Grove, Illinois, with her husband, her son, a collie, and three cats.

Acknowledgments
The photographs on the following pages are reproduced with the permission of: page 8 (left), Greater Farmington Chamber of Commerce, Farmington, Maine; pages 8–9 (center), The Franklin *Journal*, Farmington, Maine; pages 12 & 13 (baseball bats), Andy King; page 47, Airplane Kite Company.